Painting the Spectrum Gold

Advancements in Autism

Dedication

I hold a copious amount of respect for the researchers that have dedicated their lives to autism, the award winning first class geniuses that made all the research in this book possible. Without them we wouldn't have any clue about the dozen or so types of treatments that are used by parents these days, any of the medications we use, etc. Thing is, no matter the respect I hold for them, my true heroes are the mothers and fathers of the autistic adults.

These are the parents that fought this battle when medical science made autism the mother's fault, when doctors said there was no hope. The parents that sat and hoped to see any one of the research studies in this book spoke about when their children were small. Those women that stood every night, looking in the mirror wondering if maybe they did do something wrong but kept fighting for their babies none the less and the fathers that stood behind them telling them they did everything right.

Now decades later these ladies and gentlemen have become counselors to the newly diagnosed mommies and daddies. They are sources of wisdom and light. They are exactly what I hope to have the strength left in me to grow into through the next 10 years of my son and my lives.

Thank you ladies, Thank you gentlemen.

You are my heroes: This book is dedicated to you.

Painting the Spectrum Gold

Advancements in Autism

Brooke Price

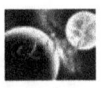

Another World Publishing   Washington

Copyright 2014

Also From Brooke Price:

-'Living Through Autism's Eyes: My Journey with My Son, 2nd Edition'

-'8 Simple Steps to IEP Success'

-'Beautiful Disasters, A Look Inside of Bipolar Disorder'

-'Redefining Normal: A Real World Guide to Raising an Autistic Child'

-'Melting Down Meltdowns: When a Tantrum isn't a Tantrum'

Painting the Spectrum Gold:

Advancements in Autism

Table of Contents

Chapter 1

Finding Truth

I t seems that when your child is diagnosed with autism that the whole world has changed with one doctor's appointment. Whether expected or not the diagnosis is still a shock to every one of us. Now you have to figure out how to redefine your life. Question is: How are you supposed to do that when it seems the world either wants to pity you, zone you out, or approach your child with inconceivable ignorance? Not to mention a lot of the information out there is actually misinformation and the doctors who treat our children know less about their disorder than we do.

Many parents find themselves surfing the web all night--trying to find answers, some truth, beyond what they're getting from doctors; just searching for something to cling onto. Others' find themselves buying every piece of literature they can find that merely mentions the word 'autism'. While these channels are very integral parts of understanding, coping, and loving autism you must also acknowledge that you can't learn much about any disorder if doctors and researchers don't know much about it themselves. Without their input, research, and time it's impossible for the world to know where science is headed.

 My son was diagnosed many years ago (2007), he was four and nonverbal at that time. His diagnosis was devastating to me despite the fact I saw it coming. When I inquired as to how my child could have autism there were not many scenarios discussed in detail with me, instead I was

told that it was believed that the mother's lack of bonding with the infant was behind it.

Luckily they do not say this to parents anymore; however that doesn't change the fact that 1000's of mothers, including myself (for only a full year after his diagnosis, then the refrigerator mom theory was abandoned), were told that over the years. Since then a great number of advances have been made in the understanding, treatment, and genetics of autism, still not enough though.

Every day our knowledge of this disorder augments. A lot of the old questions have been answered, for example: It's always been heavily debated whether children developed autism as a result of their mother smoking during pregnancy. We know the answer to that question now, it will be discussed later in this book.

In the past 7 years there have been medications tested, diets tried, networks started, genes tested, things changed, countless research studies concluded, and mass amounts of hope spread to the parents of these amazing children. Let's take a look into some of the advancements in and changes to autism.

Advancements in Autism

(Unique to this Book Pieces and Expansions on Brooke's Previously Published Works)

Chapter 2

What's in a Name?

Redefining the Severities of the Spectrum

F irst and foremost the changes in the descriptive names on the DSM-5 must be talked about. If you have not heard about these changes it's something that will affect your life, at least until it is changed again, as things typically do in the world of Autism. Some parents love the idea, some despise the very mention of it; some doctors love it and some advocate fiercely against the changes. (Before name changes are spoken of it has to be said that there were many other changes to the DSM-5 pertaining to Autism, as well as many other disorders. This chapter is based only on the descriptive name changes).

As a mother of an autistic child I'm first to admit that a great deal of parents of autistic children do not like change of any kind. We aren't particularly used to it so we shy from it; this topic is not an exclusion for most. One thing that must be remembered is

Picture Courtesy of Bing Images

that there is good reason for change sometimes, you just have to be open to it.

The Old Way

The DSM-IV is what most parents are used to, as well as a majority of doctors. It is comfortable and offers a great deal of visual recognition as to what you are diagnosed with or reading about. The DSM-IV has the autism severities broken down into 5 basic categories:

DSM-IV Autism Severities:

-Severe Autism

-Moderate Autism

-Asperger's Syndrome

-Mild Autism

-P.D.D.N.O.S.

Severe Autism

Severe Autism is referred to as "Low Functioning Autism" by some and as "Autism Level 3" to others; is an autistic child with severe social and cognitive deficits. They tend to show more sensory activities such as: spinning, rocking, and/or hand flapping. A great deal of the time children on the severe end of the spectrum don't respond to CBT [Cognitive Behavioral Therapy]; when they do they rarely show any significant improvements. Some of these children do not have a way to communicate or will not attempt to unless they have to; they also tend to show little emotions—other than anger. Some show every range of emotion known to man.

Every autistic child is different. You cannot anticipate the same symptoms, results, or treatments from one child to the other. Severely Autistic children seem to have rather high incidents of epilepsy as well as other disorders. They tend to have a heightened report of self-injury and aggression than the other degrees of severity. (Low Functioning Autism , n.d.)

Other Problems that They May Display Are:

-Impulsiveness

-Preferring to be alone

-Lack of eye contact

-Not being able to control self

-Over or under sensitivity to smell, sound, touch, pain, etc.

-Possibly not seeking comfort from parents

-Sleep Disturbances (Mild or Severe)

       (Low Functioning Autism , n.d.)

Mild Autism

Mild Autism is a child with near average IQ but still shows signs of being on the spectrum. A Mildly Autistic child has deficits, much like the other severities, but, their deficits are nowhere near as acute. These children tend to have impairments in motor skills [however nowhere near as bad as a Severely Autistic child]. Catching a ball, writing or simply tying their shoes can be particularly hard. They can still suffer from sensory issues like the other severities and they may still show repetitive speech in daily life.

Other Things to Look For:

-Mood Swings

-Agitation Caused by Routine Changes

-Above Average Memorization Abilities

-Obsessions with Toys, Hobby's, etc.

-May Talk Excessively about One Topic

(Hughes, n.d.)

Asperger's Syndrome

Asperger's Syndrome is closely related to Autism, some doctors believe that it completely independent from the spectrum though. Children with Asperger's Syndrome have a tendency to have normal to high IQ's (77-130, 100 being average); however they have many deficits in social skills. These kids do not have verbal issues, they can communicate just fine.

Some Asperger's Syndrome Symptoms:

-One Sided Relationships with "Friends"

-Problem Reading the Emotions of Others

-Problems Engaging Others in Conversations

-Clumsy Gestures

-Unaware of Personal Space of Others

-Typically Having Problems Looking in Faces

-Awkward Social Relationships

-Unable to Send Information Through Their Eyes

-Emotional Detachment from Others

(22 Main Autism Symptoms, n.d.)

PDD-NOS/ASD-NOS

PDD-NOS (Pervasive Developmental Disorder Not Otherwise Specified) is a disorder that children are diagnosed with if they show some of the signs of Autism but not all of them. These children, like any other child with a developmental disorder, are each different. No two are ever the same. Their disorder can also be broken down into severity levels; there are children with more serious impairments than other children with PDD-NOS. There are also PDD-NOS children that are very mild, they might only show a few problems at home.

A lot of parents with Autistic children scoff at parents of children with PDD-NOS, like it's a contest. Let it be known that it is not, some of the issues that some of these children have are absolutely debilitating.

Other Symptoms to Look for in PDD-NOS:

-Not understanding Friendships

-Problems understanding Others Moods

-GI Problems

-Language Delays in Some Incidents

-Sleep Disturbances

(PDD-NOS Signs, Symptoms, and Treatment, n.d.)

That's the way parents and science have looked at autism for years. This is not how they are looking at them anymore. The new way does not include 5 severities like the DSM-IV does, instead it encompasses 3.

The New Way

In an effort to more globally amalgamate research, diagnosis, and understanding of the autism spectrum researchers looked at the ICD-10 and the impending ICD-11 (equivalent to the DSM in the U.S.). The problem is that there are such demarcating differences in the two, even down to things as simple as the definitions of autism; that problem leads to the inability to properly unite work. The problem with that effort seems to be that while the new DSM has simplified to 3 types the ICD (International Classification of Diseases) currently lists the spectrum as 8 types. The other reason for these changes are the vast differences in diagnosis in the U.S. It has been said that what a child is diagnosed with and how their autism is treated depends on where in the U.S. you live and what insurance you have. Some insurances won't even recognize PDD-NOS.

Picture Courtesy of Bing Images

Changes to the DSM-5:

Autism is no longer severe, moderate, mild, Asperger's, PDD-NOS; instead the severities are listed as:

-Autism Level 3

-Autism Level 2

-Autism Level 1

Asperger's and PDD-NOS have been removed from the spectrum and intertwined with *Autism Level 2 and Level 1*. As you can imagine a lot of parents are mad about these changes. As previously mentioned, many doctors believe Asperger's is a different condition entirely, such as a genetic or developmental disorder that is not associated with autism. Given this fact you can understand their anger over this topic.

This author will say that there is a great deal of understanding for these parents position. Children with Asperger's Syndrome and PDD-NOS are exceptionally special in ways that shouldn't be abolished to a numbered category; on the flip side, a new way of defining these children is way overdue.

(Price, What's in a name? Changes in Autism Severity, 2014)

Chapter 3

Could the Answers to Autism be Found Hidden within Nasal Spray?

S cientist have been talking about the SOARS-B research study [centered out of several institutes' in several states] for some time now. The study is aimed at seeing whether the Oxytocin

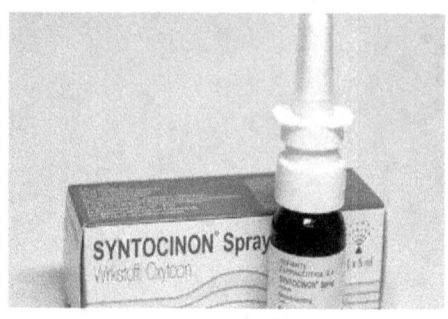

Picture of Oxytocin Nasal Spray; Courtesy of: (Conneely, n.d.)

Nasal Spray will help in treating autism. The start of these talks date back to 2008 when Autism Speaks gave up near $380,000 to Hebrew University in Jerusalem. They were charged with researching the effects of oxytocin levels in a mother prior to birth and then the use of synthetic oxytocin in infants and rating the overall correlation; if there was one to be found. After the results of the findings Autism Speaks turned around and gave the University of North Carolina $119,000 to start the first trial of oxytocin pertaining to autism. Since then they have funded countless other studies, all having fairly good results.

The SOARS-B study is the more recent research study into this potential treatment. The study was launched in 2013 when researchers were given a $12.6 million dollar grant from the U.S. Government. The name stands for: Study of Oxytocin in Autism to improve Reciprocal Social Behaviors. (Researchers launch study with oxytocin nasal spray, n.d.)

SOARS-B is following 300 autistic children; for half of the study half of the children are given Oxytocin Nasal Spray and half a placebo. The second half of the study all the children are given the Oxytocin Nasal Spray. The results are unknown as of late.

Institutes involved in this study are:

-The University of North Carolina ASPIRE program- Chapel Hill and Durham

-The Lurie Center for Autism at Massachusetts General Hospital—Boston

-Seaver Autism Center at Mount Sinai School of Medicine—New York

-Seattle Children's Research Institute—Washington

-The Vanderbilt Treatment and Research Institute for Autism Spectrum Disorders—Nashville

(Researchers launch study with oxytocin nasal spray, n.d.)

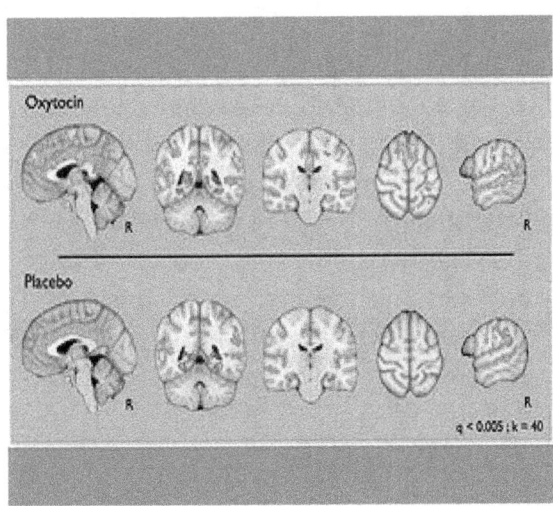

fMRI of increased brain activity when oxytocin is used (top) vs. a placebo (bottom) Picture Courtesy of: (Brooks, 2012) via Ilanit Gordon, PhD, Yale University, New Haven, Connecticut

The one thing that makes this study and potential treatment so exciting is the luck that has been seen in other studies involving Oxytocin. Example: Stanford University was recently able to prove an association between Oxytocin and Serotonin levels in one's brain. Essentially they were able to show that oxytocin influences the levels of serotonin. (Gul Dolen, 2012)

When contacted for comment about the Oxytocin Nasal Spray trial, Angela Sirigu, PhD of the Institute of Cognitive Science, Centre de Neuroscience Cognitive, Lyon, France, said she believes the findings of the study to be "interesting since they confirm our previous results obtained on adult Asperger patients we published in PNAS in 2010, and they also show that therapeutic potential of oxytocin can also be extended to children" (Brooks, 2012)

The PNAS study had 13 adult volunteers that were given oxytocin to inhale. At the end of the study they found that the oxytocin was highly beneficial in treating adults with Asperger's Syndrome. Not only did the volunteers have better response time and ability to understand in simulated ball toss games but they also showed to have increased the amount of time the adults could "zone out" into a picture, particularly around the eye area of the picture. This was a placebo-controlled study that's findings show, yet another, link between oxytocin and autism. (Brooks, 2012)

All this boils down to researchers having the ability to say that oxytocin increasing serotonin levels sends a shock wave of hope through the scientific community. They are able to say that there is a notable connection between oxytocin and being able to make social interactions easier for autistic children through the use of this nasal spray.

The Claims of Researchers about Oxytocin Nasal Spray:

-Increase Child's Ability to Recognize Emotions of Others

-Social Memory Increased

-Lowering Repetitive Behaviors and Scripting

-Lessen Social Anxiety

These symptoms are claimed to be helped within 3 weeks of treatment—their base claim is that Oxytocin Nasal Spray will help treat the "core symptoms" of autism. The flip side to this potential treatment is that there actually are other studies out there that suggest that this course of treatment would be entirely ineffective. In these studies it's been found that there's no improvements in emotional recognition, social skills, repetitive behaviors, or in general when using the nasal spray. (No oxytocin benefit for autism, 2013)

Another point to always remember is that there will always be side effects that come along with any treatment.

Side Effects Associated with Oxytocin Nasal Spray:

-Runny Nose

-Irritation of the Inside of the Nose

-Excessive Eye Watering

-Mental Disorder with Loss of Normal Personality and Reality

-Seizures

-Bleeding Not Related to a Menstrual Period

-Uterine Contractions

(Drugs & Medications, n.d.)

There's definitely more that needs to be understood in regards to this potential treatment, but you have to admit the thought of it working is exhilarating.

(Price, Will oxytocin nasal spray treatments for autism really work? , 2014)

Chapter 4

The Unheard of "Miracle Medication"

O xytocin Nasal Spray is not the only medication currently being studied to aid in the treatment of autism. Studies into the use of Arbaclofen [derived of Bacofen], a medicine used to treat muscle spasms are showing promise. Many scientist believe that when compared to the Oxytocin spray study the Arbaclofen shows incalculable improvements in tackling the "core symptoms" of autism. There are presently two studies into the use of this medicine. One being a clinical trial on children with Fragile X syndrome, the other is a mouse study.

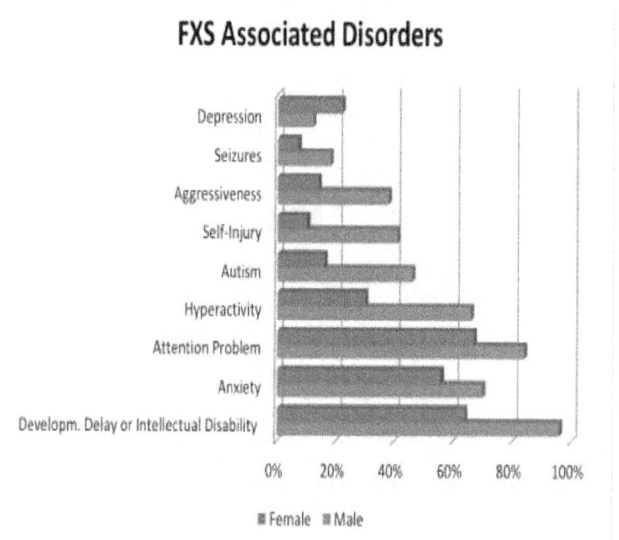

CoMorbid Disorders of Fragile X Syndrome. Picture Courtesy of: (Negro, n.d.)

A problem most parents notice and all doctors know is that there are no medications proven to work in helping reduced the real symptoms seen in our children; let alone that are approved for use in children. Typically the medications currently used are more to cope with the anger and speech issues that these children face. Solving those issues seems to be an aim of both studies.

The Mice Study

In the mice study the researchers took their mice and essentially turned off their FMR1 gene. Common people do not need to know about genetic mutations and so on, so a great deal of people have no idea what this gene is, what is caused by issues with this gene, or what happens whenever this gene is muted? This author certainly had no clue what the FMR1 gene was or what to expect from a mutation of it.

It's suggested that the autistic brain has a habit of overproducing a particular protein called glutamate. When the FMR1 gene is muted the brain loses the mRNA translational repressor protein resulting in Fragile X mental retardation proteins, or FMRP. Once the gene is muted the mice are said to begin showing Fragile X Syndrome. From this point it's like a domino effect. (Reversal of disease-related pathologies in fragile x mouse model by selectve activation of GABAB receptors with arbaclofen, 2012)

How things unfold once the FMR1 gene is muted:

-Brain cells lose their ability to respond to the Neurotransmitter Gluamate

-Once this happens the cells begin to overproduce some proteins

-The end result is deformities in the dendritic spine (connectors between brain cells, receives information)

-All these changes cause Fragile X Syndrome in children (Reversal of disease-related pathologies in fragile x mouse model by selectve activation of GABAB receptors with arbaclofen, 2012)

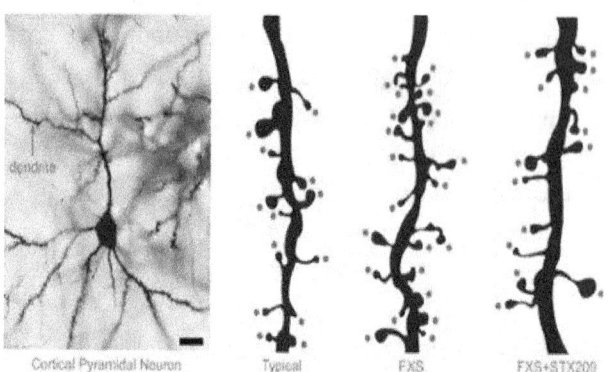

Second picture from left is a typical dendritic spine; Third from the left is one of a fragile x mouse; Picture on far right is the dendritic spines of fragile x mice after treated with arbaclofen Picture Courtesy of: (Arbaclofen Shows Promise for Treating Core Symptoms of Autism, 2012)

Fragile X Syndrome can cause several deficits in children. These deficits range anywhere from learning to behavior, even to sensory. It's not an easy disorder to live with nor is it easy to raise; however they are certainly some of the easiest kids to love.

Some Common Symptoms of Fragile X Syndrome (every child is different):

-Learning Issues that Range from the Extreme End of Mild to the Extreme End of Severe

-Speech and Language Impairments; stuttering, etc.

-Boys are more likely to have Speech Impairments

-Some Fragile X Children are Nonverbal their whole lives

-Physical differences noticed toward puberty such as: Narrow Faces, Large Ears, Flat Feet, Large Heads, and a Prominent Forehead

-Boys can be Very Aggressive and Hyperactive

-Hard to Maintain Eye Contact

-Sensory issues

(What are the Symptoms of Fragile X Syndrome? , n.d.)

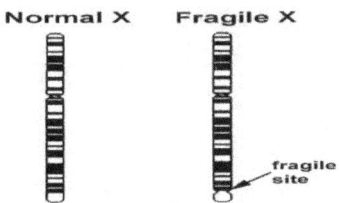

A Normal Chromosome vs A Fragile X Chromosome. Picture Courtesy of Bing Images

The mice exhibited some of the same symptoms once the FMR1 gene was muted. Their seizures seemingly stopped and the repetitive behaviors that they were showing lessened. Not only that but the proteins in their brains regulate and the cells were able to communicate properly. (Reversal of disease-related pathologies in fragile x mouse model by selectve activation of GABAB receptors with arbaclofen, 2012)

The Clinical Trial of Individuals with Fragile X Syndrome:

The aim of this study is, of course, to see what the effects of Arbaclofen is on individuals with Fragile X Syndrome and how it may relate to autism. The findings were rather thought-provoking, especially if you look at the amount of shared "core symptoms" there are between the two disorders.

In this "double blind" study researchers took 63 individuals ages 6-39 years that had a complete FMR1 gene mutation; 55 of the 63 where male. During this placebo-controlled study the individuals were given arbaclofen then closely watched and tested to determine whether there were any definitive improvements in behavior. (EM, 2012) By the end of this study it was determined that there were not significant improvements noted for individuals using this medication; however when they took a side group of individuals that would fit into the severe end of the disorders and tried this with them the results were quite different than with the first study.

After being given arbaclofen the individuals with more severe deficits showed an improvement on all global measures, these results were the same for the entire group of 27 used for the post-study. The individuals were tested with the Vineland II-Socialization raw score and with the ABC-Social Avoidance scale both showing improvement. (EM, 2012).

The only documented side effects with using arbaclofen are upper respiratory infections (13%), headaches (8%), and deep sleep in 8% of patients. (Therapeutics, n.d.) One other thing pertaining to Fragile X Syndrome mentioned in this study was that this medication does not help with the irritability shown by some children with Fragile X Syndrome. (EM, 2012) Overall the findings of these studies prove to be promising, definitely a step in the right direction for sure. As with most new medications, therapies, or doctors, more research is needed before a definite commitment is given to trying it when available.

Chapter 5

Using Cannabis to Treat Autism; Is this the Answer?

n an effort to advance science sometimes looks to areas that make the general public choleric. If you're an individual with abhorrence for "thinking outside the box" then I can assure you the direction researchers are leaning, in regards to THC as an autism treatment, is really going to agitate you.

The Studies

Sparking Everyone's Interest

In 2012 Dr. Daniele Piomelli, of the University of California Irvine and Dr. Olivier Manzoni of INSERM (French National Research Agency) with collaboration from Hungry and Italy, led this study which identified compounds that inhibit enzymes blocking endocannabinoid transmitters [called 2-AG in the striatum and cortex regions] of the brain. These specific transmitters allow for transport of electrical signals at synapses. (UCI)

Essentially what scientists did was take "Fragile X mice" and treat them with endocannabinoid compounds that correct the endocannabinoid transmitters in their brains. (UCI) [Endocannabinoid compounds made in your body share a significantly similar chemical structure with THC]. Once the mice were treated with endocannabinoid compounds the "Fragile X mice" exhibited immense improvements in maze tests aimed to measure anxiety and open-space acceptance. (UCI) Overall the study points towards potential cannabis treatments for the cognitive deficits and anxiety found in autism as well as other disorders.

Endocannabinoids and Autism:

A 2013 Stanford University Study looking into the different affects certain genetic mutations related to autism have on the brain of mice resulted in findings they didn't expect. The 2013 Nobel Prize in Physiology or Medicine co-awardee- Prof. Thomas Sudhof, Dr. Csasa Foldy, and 2010 Goldman-Rakic Prize in Neuroscience winner- Dr. Robert Malenka all set out to acquire a further understanding of how various mutations in the brain may or may not contribute to autism. They focused their study on two types of NL3 neuroligin mutations (NL3 KO and R451C KI) with a few main goals in mind; two expressly:

-Find a mutual phenotype between the two different NL3 mutations

-Test if NL3 KO and R451C KI mutations cause different phenotypes, even in divergent synapses on the same neuron. (Thomas Sudhof, 2013)

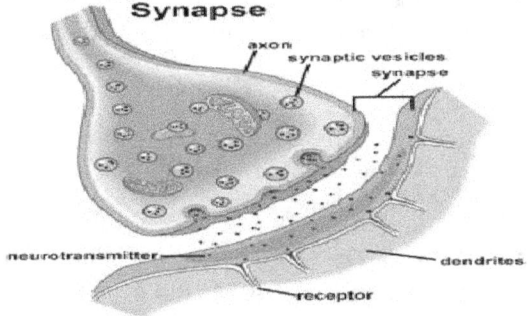

Photo Courtesy of Google Images, also Nanotechnology and Neuroscience

While looking at the NL3 KO mutated mice they noticed their tonic endocannabinoid signaling was disrupted, as were they in the R451C KI mutated mice. These finding are exciting: before this study researchers knew so little about tonic endocannabinoids that their existence as an unambiguous process was actually unclear. (Thomas Sudhof, 2013) Given this phenotype is found in both mutations of the NL3 neuroligins used [NL3 KO and R451C KI] this clearly shows that the NL3 molecule is the very first known molecule essential for tonic endocannabinoid signaling, subsequently substantiating the fact that tonic endocannabinoids aren't "accidental" transient endocannabinoid leakages. (Thomas Sudhof, 2013) This also gives strong credence to the theory that loss of endocannabinoid signaling may be a component to autism.

When the researchers shifted focus to the RC451C KI mutated mice they were strongly motivated to prove R451C KI mutations can cause "loss of function" much like what is seen in autism. (Thomas Sudhof, 2013) They were irrefutably able to prove this theory enabling them to say that autism may be caused by a disruption in the child's brain's ability to send clear communications; strongly suggesting that cannabinoids, such as THC, may be productively used in treating autism [by unblocking the disruptions].

Bringing the Research to Life:

Believe it or not 14 states now allow cannabis use in children. One California mother has become a pioneer in the use of cannabis in children. Her courage has given parents the courage to speak out eventually creating a movement that no one saw coming. Not only that but there was a bill sent to the House of Representatives on July 21, 2014 proposing changes to the Controlled Substance Act. They are aiming to make exceptions for marijuana that has low THC counts. This will be particularly important to this predominantly parental movement. If passed it gives cogency to their claims that this "drug" has caused the improvements they see in their children as well as it showing the 22 states that currently allow medical marijuana that the government's paying attention.

Improvements Seen from Cannabis use in Autistic Children:

-Improved Sleep

-Diminished Hyperactivity

-Minimized Irritability

-Decreased Stereotypy

-Diminution in Seizures

-Decrease in Violent Outbursts

-Minimized Inappropriate Speech

-Initiating Physical Contact

-Improved appetite

(Thomas Sudhof, 2013)

Of course the mental image of an autistic child smoking a joint is incommodious; you'll be relieved to find out that's not how they administer cannabis to children. There are two active ingredients in cannabis: THC and CBD. Either type can be administered numerous ways.

Administering Cannabis to Children:

-Edibles (Brownies, muffins, suckers, etc.)

-Drinks (Tea, Lemonade, Soda, etc.)

-Honey Sticks

-Capsules

-Oils and Lotions

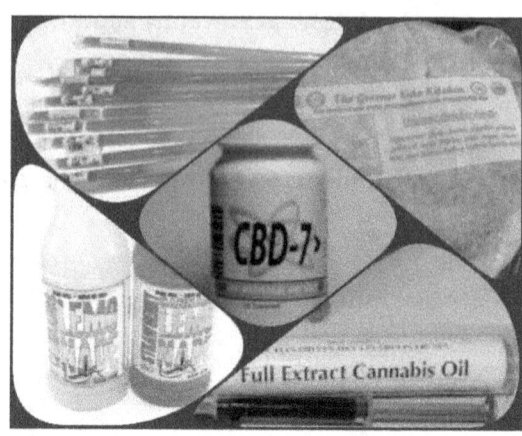

There are other studies on medications relevant to cannabis use in autism worth citing, Dronabinol and Epidiolex. Dronabinol is a THC based medication given to chemotherapy and AIDS patients to battle weight loss and loss of appetite. (Plus) In autistic children it has shown exceptional results in all areas referred to above. Epidiolex is a CBD based medication that has shown to improve symptoms of epileptics (Gardner, 2013). Currently there are studies going looking into its effectiveness when used in autism.

Of course more research needs to be done before everyone will be comfortable with this idea, also, the side effects associated with cannabis usage need to be further researched where it pertains to children. Regardless of the unknowns a great deal of people, including me, find these studies immensely intriguing. Not because of the cannabis movement in America today, but for the reason that there are a lot of things my child suffers through and no medication has ever helped with. I've set up 7 nights a week for 11 years crying because my child won't sleep (literally), I've held my baby in basket holds while he tried his hardest to hurt himself or me-knowing he didn't care which way it went, watched my angel seize continuously having to be put into a coma to calm his body while his mind continued to seize, begged in my head for him to want to be hugged all while wishing he'd calm down, and I've cried while he struggled to speak for 6 years. He's gone through more in his 11 years than most do in their whole life, so yeah, the prospect interests me as a parent in an impossible situation with a child that few understand.

The principal arguments made in opposition to this treatment are the side effects and potential for addiction. As I see it, a vast majority of medications used to treat autistic children aren't approved for use in minors; a great deal don't help or have preposterous side effects and some are addicting as well (all ostensibly worse [to me] than the side effects concomitant with cannabis use). It seems that, perhaps, it's time we open our minds to other approaches since most of the treatments we have now aren't up to par.

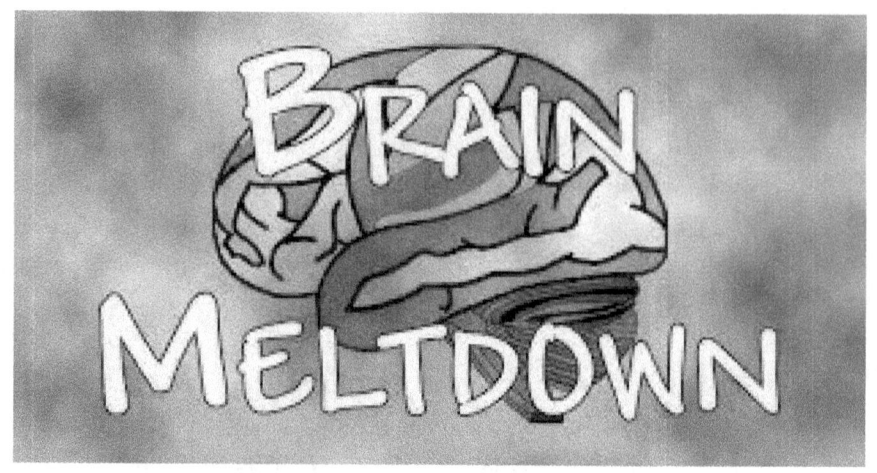

Picture Courtesy of meltdownmentor.com

Chapter 6

The Much Debated "Autism Diet"

The "Autism Diet", as it's called by some, is one of the most heavily debated topics in the autism community. The only more heated topics of discussion are the "Vaccine Debate" and the "Cause/Cure Debate". Some parents swear by it and some laugh at it; it is recommended by some doctors and others will tell you it's a waste of time.

The Gluten Free or the Gluten Free Casein Free Diets are newest "fad" amongst health freaks and their followers. Before that it was most commonly used by individuals with Celiac Disease. This disease makes it very painful for a person to take ingest gluten. However a lot of people hadn't heard of it being used for autism treatment until somewhat recently.

The Parental Side:

Despite what they're told some parents swear their child or children process their food differently than most. They believe that this difference in food processing makes their child's autism worse. Another belief by some is that their child's body treats peptides like a "deceptive opiate-like chemical", the reaction to this is believed to cause their child's autism.

A great deal of parents will elect to have blood work done to prove a gluten allergy. Most are told their child has no such allergy; in turn the parent will go about their business like they never heard the results.

Benefits Reported by Parents from using the Gluten Free Diet:

-Executive Functioning Improvements

-Maladaptive Behaviors Improvements

-Meltdowns Lessened

-Sleep Disturbances more Neutralized

-Social Behavior Improved

-Speech Improved

-Their Child is "Cured"

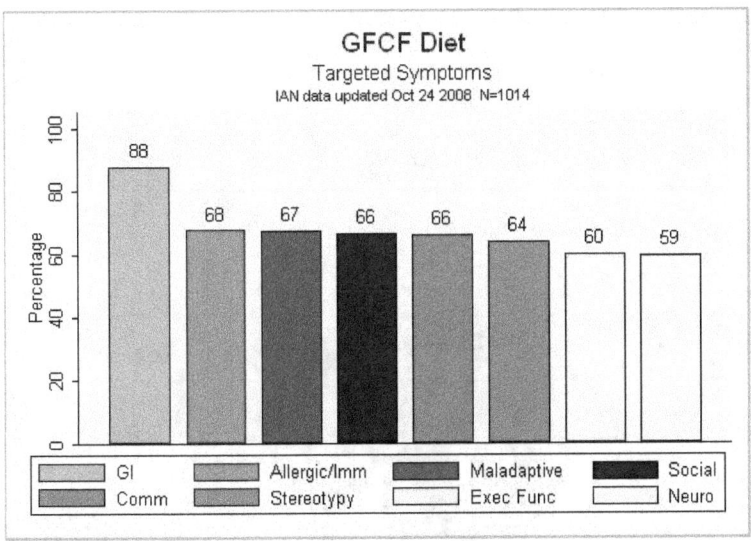

Symptoms that are targeted by the GFCF diet. Picture Courtesy of: (IanProject, 2008)

While parents who use the GF diet with their child advocate strongly for it when speaking to other parents, they do have vastly differing expectations on what they are going to be able

to achieve via the diet. Their expectations, as logged by Ian
Project, are more on the minimal to moderate range.

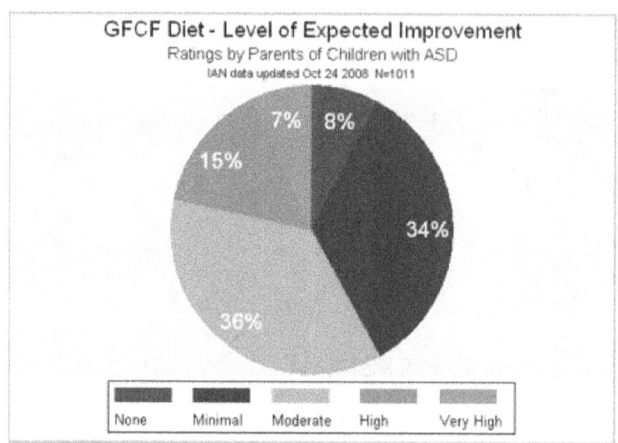

Expectation of Parents of Autistic Children. Picture Courtesy of: (IanProject,
2008)

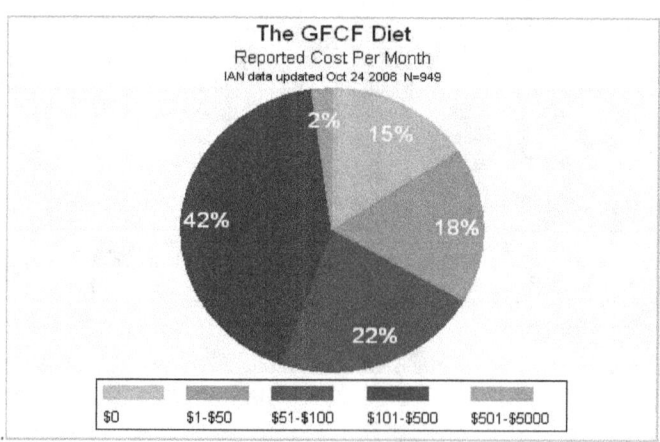

Parental reported monthly costs for the GF diet. Picture Courtesy of:
(IanProject, 2008)

If all of those results are accurate than they certainly would offset the (Ian Project, 2008) expenses associated with the Gluten Free Diet, specifically the change in grocery prices for families. On average this diet costs a family $100-$500 extra to maintain monthly

The Scientific Side:

What stance you take concerning this diet in the professional world is entirely reflective of where in the world you are. U.S. researchers are fairly in agreement that there is no help from this diet for autistic children unless they have a GI issue; overseas however there is more support for it.

The opinions of researchers in the U.S. are extremely different that a lot of the parents of autistic children. It seems doctors and researchers really enjoy being on the opposite side of the fence; however they will acknowledge that half of all autistic child also have some sort of gastrointestinal issue and that a majority of pain receptors are found in the stomach.

If you look at Danish researchers though you see scientist that tell you that the GF diet shows significant results in treating some autistic children. (NLM, n.d.) The Danish study followed the children for 2 years where the U.S. studies average about 3 months following the children.

While it was mentioned before that they GF diet costs a bit more monthly to be on, it also has very strict rules you have to adhere to.

Foods You Cannot Eat While on the Gluten Free Diet:

Ingredient No-No's:

-Rye, rye flour, pumpernickel flour, or any form of the word rye.

-Oats, oatmeal, oat flour, oat groats, or any form of the word oats, if your doctor has advised you to avoid oats. If your doctor permits oats on your gluten-free diet, look for gluten-free oats

-Flour, including instant, bread, cake, enriched, graham, and all-purpose flours. Flours made from safe grains (such as corn flour, millet flour, and rice flour) are safe.

-Malt, unless specified as being made from a non-gluten source (such as corn).

-Wheat, wheat berries, wheat bran, wheat germ, wheatgrass, or any form of the word wheat

-Barley, barley malt, barley flour, or any form of the word barley

-Triticale

-Einkorn

-Spelt

-Semolina

-Durum

-Bulgar or Bulghar

-Kamut

-Cracker meal

-Couscous

-Tabbouleh

-Tempura crumbs

(Groce, 2014)

Food No-No's:

-Hydrolyzed vegetable protein

-Modified food starch

-Vegetable starch or vegetable protein

-Gelatinized starch or pregelatinized starch

-Natural flavorings

-Soy sauce

-Breads, pastries, cakes, cookies, crackers, doughnuts, pies, pretzels, and all other baked goods

-Breakfast cereals, both hot and cold

-Pasta, including gnocchi, spaetzle, chow mein, lo mein, and filled pastas

-Snack foods, especially if seasoned or highly processed.

Picture Courtesy of Bing Images

-Soups, gravies, and thickened sauces

-Breaded meats or vegetables, such as fried chicken or okra

-Dumplings, meatballs, lunch meats, meat loaves, and similar foods (often held together with breadcrumbs or flour).

-Beer

-Salad dressings, Worcestershire sauce, and other condiments

(Groce, 2014)

Maybe in a few years this diet will be more widely accepted by doctors and parents. The current information available is still somewhat sketchy, but then again, what information do we have about autism that isn't still a bit sketchy?

(Price, Does the Gluten Free-Casein Free Diet Have a Place in the Autism Community?, 2014)

Chapter 7

The Autism Gene: It Really Does Exist

To quote Raphael Bernier, one of the researchers involved in this autism advancement "This will be a game changer in the way scientists are researching autism". That it will be.

Researchers from the *Autism Center at Seattle Children's* took 6,176 kids with autism and did genetic studies with them. Of the 6,176 children 15 had a mutation called a CHD8 mutation. All 15 children are said to have sleep disturbances, intestinal issues, and similar facial characteristics.

To further prove there was a link there researchers had scientists from *Duke University* inject the CHD8 gene into fish embryos. To everyone's amazement when the fish were born they had incongruous characteristics, as they aged they acquired intestinal problems. (Raphael Bernier, 2014)

What does this mean?

Scientist finally found a definite autism specific gene that isn't a CNV. This discovery is huge, while the potential of occurrence is very rare. This still means that doctors may not have to treat our children in the same sort of pattern; just with different drugs. Parents may not ever have to leave the appointment where their child is diagnosed with more questions than they went into the appointment with. Maybe this discovery will eventually lead to all these things and some actual answers that we can all agree on.

The Science behind this Discovery:

Autism is one of those disorders that is mostly diagnosed by observation of the child's behaviors as reported by the child's parents, teachers, and the doctor themselves. The doctor will also do many tests with you to determine if your child does fit the textbook *"autism spectrum disorder"* diagnosis. The problem is that very little of the testing is actually done with the child, because in most cases the autistic child will have some sort of speech issue, most of the testing is actually done with the parent simply answering questions.

Scientist do know of some genetic occurrences that pertain to autism, such as Fragile X. The difference is that these genetic occurrences are caused by CNV's or a Copy Number Variation's. A CNV is when sections of a person's DNA is copied or possibly deleted. (Iyer, 2014) No scientists have been able to prove an absolute connection between any CNV and autism. They know they frequently see autism on these "hot spot" markers; in the world of science it's all about what you can prove though.

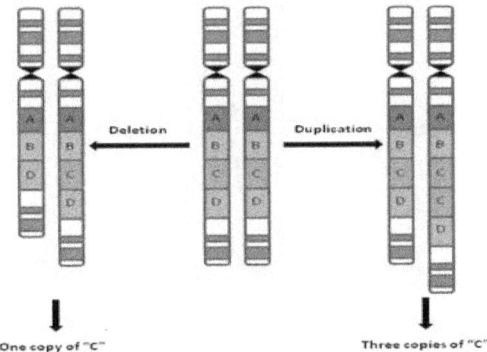

Deletion and Duplication of Chromosomes, called: Copy Number Variation's Picture Courtesy of: (2013, n.d.)

The belief is that the discovery of this gene mutation will allow for our children to be diagnosed based on medical facts, on the actual underlying conditions, can you imagine being able to go to the doctor with your child and get answers that day? Answers that made sense and were universal no matter what doctor you saw? Wouldn't it be odd at first to be able to go to the doctor and be given actual sound advice as to what to do from there? Currently we do not have these luxuries; furthermore, doctors are currently fighting among themselves just as much as they are fighting the parents they should be learning from.

One of the most exciting points of this finding is that researchers say from here they will eventually be able to develop different drugs for each subtype of autism they find. (Iyer, 2014)

(Price, Cause for autism sub-type found: what does this mean for parents? , 2014)

Chapter 8

Tracing the Untraceable

I n 2000 the President Bill Clinton and the U.S. government put through the **Children's Health Act of 2000**--the intent of said act was/is to further understand the scope of Autism in our country. With this in place the CDC (Center for Disease Control) was able to start up a *"network"* to better monitor and understand autism; they call it the *"**Autism and Developmental Disabilities Monitoring [ADDM] Network**"*. (CDC, CDC's Autism and Developmental Disabilities Monitoring (ADDM) Network, n.d.)

ADDM was and is a very exciting step towards understanding how the autism prevalence is growing; even if being monitored isn't exactly your *"cup of tea"*. **ADDM** aids researchers in spotting spot trends in prevalence increase. **ADDM** is the only collaboration intent on not only tracking the characteristics of autism, but, the numbers as well. (CDC, Autism and Developmental Disabilities Monitoring (ADDM) Network, 2014)

ADDM has been performing population based surveillance every other year for ASDs in the states listed below since 2000 (Kalkbrenner, 2012), they've been releasing prevalent numbers to the nation and to the parents of autistic children and adults since 2007, when their first report was published. At that time the numbers suggested that the national autism prevalence sat at approximately 1 in 150; those parents that sat there and watched them announce those findings surely cannot forget the shock and sadness that washed over us all.

Prevalence Findings by the ADDM Over the Last 7 years:

-**2014**—1 in 68 Children Identified (Based on 2010 Data)

-2012—1 in 88 Children Identified (Based on 2008 Data)

-2009—1 in 110 Children Identified (Based on 2006 Data)

-2007—1 in 150 Children Identified (Based on 2002 Data)

(CDC, Autism and Developmental Disabilities Monitoring (ADDM) Network, 2014)

These numbers show that since 2002, when they started taking data, the autism prevalence has risen **123%**. Quite an absurd increase in percentage by any standards.

How do They Come Up with the Numbers?

The way that these prevalence numbers are calculated is not the way most would expect them to be. Generally people seem to think that the data is taken from all over the U.S. and averaged out, or split into categories and analyzed. ADDM Network simplifies the process and still predicts prevalence numbers; who you are depends highly on your belief in the reliability of their findings.

ADDM has sat up *"Monitoring Stations"* across 14 states, as of 2014. These serve as monitoring posts for autism activity in that particular area; focusing on 8 year old children diagnosed with autism. (CDC, CDC's Autism and Developmental Disabilities Monitoring (ADDM) Network, n.d.)

Locations of ADDM "Monitoring Stations":

-Alabama

-Arizona

-Arkansas

-Colorado

-Florida

-Maryland

-Missouri

-New Jersey

-North Carolina

-Pennsylvania

-South Carolina

-Utah

-West Virginia

-Wisconsin (CDC, CDC's Autism and Developmental Disabilities Monitoring (ADDM) Network, n.d.)

Current ADDM Network Sites, Surveillance Year 2012

Networking Sites used by ADDM in 2012. Picture Courtesy of: (CDC, Autism and Developmental Disabilities Monitoring (ADDM) Network, 2014)

ADDM not only gathers information about autism prevalence numbers, but, they've also been able to bring several key points to the forefront. Things such as:

- White children have a higher autism prevalence rate than Black or Hispanic kids.

-The prevalence in white children in 1 in 63, while in Black children and Asian children it's more like 1 in 81 and Hispanic children 1 in 93.

-The prevalence is higher in boys (1 in 39) than in girls (1 in 181).

-46% of children identified as having autism have average to above average IQ's.

-Give a reliable projection of how many school age ASD children

-Tell us how many children with autism are in special education classes and/or actually diagnosed by a physician. (80%), (CDC, Autism and Developmental Disabilities Monitoring (ADDM) Network, 2014)

Some parents will be thrilled to hear that there was such a network put into place and some will find a conspiracy theory wrapped up in it somewhere, this author falls somewhere in between. Where ever you stand in your support of **ADDM** all parents of disabled children realized [even before the professionals did] that this was fast becoming an *(dare the word be used)* epidemic; that a closer eye needed to be kept on the families living with autism in order to find the answers of how to treat it. Here's the Government's answer to that, in a way it seems.

(Price, Ever wondered how they come up with Autism Prevalence Numbers?, 2014)

Chapter 9

MIND:

CHARGE, APP, AND AGRE

MIND:

MIND institute is probably one of the most interesting autism driven research networks. MIND was started by 6 families in the height of their struggle with autism. We all have to admit that it is a struggle, especially in the beginning. This institute was built by these 6 families into what it is today.

Their website states: "The MIND Institute is dedicated to finding treatments, causes and preventions, and providing education for neurodevelopmental disorders. These families envisioned a place where experts from every discipline related to brain development would work together to ensure better futures for the one in twenty Americans who are affected with neurodevelopmental disorders." (MIND)

The MIND institute does research on:

-Autism Spectrum Disorders

-Fragile X Syndrome

-ADD/ADHD

-Chromosome 22q11.2 Deletion Syndrome

-Down Syndrome

(MIND)

This wonderful institute not only has the CHARGE Study, APP, and AGRE it also has the Massie Family Clinic, the Social Skills Training Program, the ADHD Clinic.

CHARGE:

CHARGE, or the Childhood Autism Risks from Genetics and the Environment, is a "comprehensive study or environmental causes and risk factors for autism and developmental delay. It is ran by the MIND Institute out of Sacramento, CA. This amazing network was launched in 2003 and was the first of its kind, in fact they were the first to identify a link between our genes and environmental causes. (CHARGE)

The researchers associated with CHARGE are:

-Irva Hetrz-Picciotto, PhD

-Robin Hansen, MD

-Judy Van de Water, PhD

-Peter Green, PhD

-Jeff Gregg, MD

-Frank Sharp, MD

-Isaac Pessah, PhD

And they are sponsored by:

-National Institute of Environmental Health Sciences

-U.S. Environmental Protection Agency

-MIND Institute

-Autism Speaks

-The Allen Foundation

-Cure Autism Now

-National Institute for Occupational Safety and Health

Charge has brought us research studies such as:

-Maternal metabolic conditions and risk for autism and other neurodevelopmental disorders

-Maternal influenza or fever during pregnancy associated with autism or developmental delays

-Tipping the balance of autism risk: Potential mechanisms linking pesticides and autism

-Autism spectrum disorders in Hispanics and non-Hispanics

-Parental Occupational exposures and autism spectrum disorders

-Month of conception and risk of autism (CHARGE)

ETC.

This network is only open to children that were born in California though. Your child must also be between 24 and 60 months of age, have English or Spanish speaking parents, and live with at least one of their biological parents. There is an evaluation to be accepted. (CHARGE)

APP:

APP, or the Autism Phenome Project, is "the largest and most comprehensive assessment of children with autism ever attempted. It aims to distinguish among recognized subgroups or phenotypes of autism. It will link these different forms of autism with distinct patterns of behavior and biological changes" (APP) The eligibility to participate is the same as it is with CHARGE.

APP was started back in 2006. It includes 55 children and their families and over 53 MIND scientists from eight research areas. This project has been in the design phase, as they put it, for 2 years now. In the end this study will include over 1800 children across several sites in the U.S.A. [Perhaps even internationally] This study includes children aged 2-3.5. They will be taking all data, genetic and otherwise, from this study and comparing it to typically developing children, no other details are given about the study at this time.

AGRE: The Autism Genetic Resource Exchange

This gem is a scientific venture by Autism Speaks and the National Institute of Mental Health; this repository was originally founded by CAN [Cure Autism Now] which merged in 2006. AGRE was started in 1997 and is the largest shared resources on autism in the world. They, basically, bank autistic children's DNA for use by scientists. This is an amazing resource for doctors and researchers. Currently their website says that they have a collection of over 1700 multiplex and simplex families that are available to the science community. The collection is kept in the Rutgers University Repository [RUCDR]. (AGRE)

Information kept by AGRE:

-Various Rating scale scores (ADI-R, ADOS, PPVt, Raven Coloured Progressive Matrices, Vineland, SCQ, RBS, Stanfors Binet Intelligence Scales, SRS, and a Language questionnaire

-Various Medical data such as Medical history, Handedness questionnaire, head circumference, Fragile z screening, High density SNP genotypes, Karyotyping or chromosomal analysis, Whole genome Scan

-Demographic data such as: Age, sex, race, and ethnicity

(AGRE)

If you'd like to join in AGRE has a data management system called ISAAC you can try, they also have a clinical research site called OSCR that launched in 2009 you could take a look at. No matter what part of the website you look into I beseech you to look! These networks are our lifelines as parents.

Chapter 10

Interactive Autism Network Project:

Ian Project/Ian Research/Ian Community

I f you ever have a question to look up or need to find a bit of research Ian project is a great place to start. Ian is a product of the Kennedy Krieger Institute that was established in 2006. The websites were subsequently launched nationwide in April 2007. I must say that Ian Project is one of my favorite networks launched. (Institute) My family has an Ian Research account and have had since the website launched. It is really worth the time when you know your information is going to good use.

This network provides many different services to families of autistic children all over the nation. As they claim, they have been able to help over 300 studies since launching. Researchers worldwide work with the information families provide to help to learn about the effect of factors such as genetics, environment, and treatment. (IANProject)

Even though Ian is a product, ran by Kennedy Krieger, it is funded by Autism Speaks and the Simons Foundation, along with a grant from the National Institutes of Health. At Ian their goal is to help parents of autistic children to be able to understand the research and research process easier, Keep up with the latest research, news, etc., understand the value of participating in research, and influence the direction of the research by participating. For our children: they just want to improve their lives. I tend to believe that is their goal seeing as though Kennedy Krieger's webpage's header is: "We are all born with great potential, shouldn't we all have the chance to achieve it?" (Institute)

Ian's Staff include:

-Dr. Paul Lipkin

-Dr. Kiely Law

-Cheryl Cohen

-Dr. Jay Nestle

-Dr. Alison Marvin

-Tara Zandi

-Mariana Sarris

-Elisabeth Arthur

-Bryan Stark

Ian also keeps a "bank" of useful information that is provided by us parents by completely surveys and keeping our family pages up to date. Again I beg of you to look into the Ian research program. It's hard to comprehend how important it is for you to sit there and complete survey after survey and update medical files every couple of months but it's WORTH it!

interactive
autism network
IANproject.org

Chapter 11

The Age Old Question:

Can Maternal Smoking Cause Autism?

One of the most heavily debated potential causes is maternal smoking. For years now the credibility of the theory concerning maternal smoking and autism has been questioned. There's been studies that prove there's a correlation between maternal smoking and behavioral disorders leading most to believe that it must have something to do with autism. The number one question that everyone has is if there's a tangible connection between autism and maternal smoking? Well here are two collaborative studies

Photo Courtesy of: fairfaxregional.com.au

that give answer to whether there are links between the two or not.

The Studies

United States Based Study:

A collaborative study between:

-Dr. Amy Kalkbrenner of the Ziber School of Public Health, University of Wisconsin-Milwaukee

-Dr. Joe Braun of the Department of Environmental Health, Harvard School of Public Health

-Dr. Maureen Durkin of the Department of Population Health Sciences, Wisconsin School of Medicine and Public Health

-Dr. Matthew Maenner of the Waisman Center, University of Wisconsin

-Dr. Christopher Cunniff of the Department of Pediatrics, University of Arizona College of Medicine

-Dr. Li-Chung Lee of the Department of Epidemiology, John Hopkins Bloomberg School of Public Health

-Dr. Sydney Pettygrove of the College of Public Health, University of Arizona

-Dr. Joyce Nicholas of the Department of Medicine, Division of Biostatistics and Epidemiology, Medical University of South Carolina

-Dr. Julie Daniels of the Department of Epidemiology, University of North Carolina at Chapel Hill

Looked into the link between maternal smoking and autism among children age 8; they used the "Autism and Developmental Disabilities Monitoring [ADDM] Network" and birth certificate databases to locate their subjects. Researchers took information about 633,989 children that lived in ADDM states. The children used for the study were all born in 1992, 1994, 1996, and 1998. Out of the 633,989 children 3,315 were autistic. (Kalkbrenner, 2012)

The locations that were used from the ADDM surveillance network included:

-5 Northern Counties in Alabama

-All of Arkansas, Miami-Dade County in Florida

-5 Counties in Metropolitan Atlanta in Georgia

-Baltimore County and the 5 Surrounding Counties in Maryland

-6 Counties in Metropolitan St. Louis in Missouri and Illinois

-Union County South of Newark in New Jersey

-10 Counties Surrounding Greensboro and Durham in North Carolina

-Philadelphia County in Pennsylvania

-5 Counties in Southeastern Wisconsin [including Milwaukee]

-All of West Virginia

In the total group of individuals used 13% of mother's smoked while pregnant, there were other very interesting statistics mentioned as well. While they are not specific to the topic at hand, they are interesting enough that I feel they should be mentioned.

Interesting Statistics:

-Non-Hispanic, married, white mother's had the highest ASD prevalence.

-Prevalence raised as the mother's age raised

-The ASD prevalence for children born to moms with college degrees was more than twice the prevalence as moms with less than a high school education.

The study showed that of the whole group of individuals that were used 13% of the total mother's smoked while pregnant. They found that the instance of smoking was the highest in mothers with low educations, unmarried, and that were fairly young at the time they had their child. (Kalkbrenner, 2012) Also that Non-Hispanic white mothers were more likely to smoke during pregnant. They also found that mothers with less than a high school education were 13 times more likely to smoke while they are pregnant. (Kalkbrenner, 2012)

In the end their results were that 11% of the source population diagnosed with classic low functioning autism had a mother that smoked throughout her pregnancy, Asperger's Syndrome and other subgroups tested basically the same. (Kalkbrenner, 2012) Both suggesting that there is no association between a child being autistic and a mother smoking during pregnancy. Interesting thing is that the study found that children diagnosed with PDD-NOS [ASD-NOS] did present with a possible correlation. There was a significant percentage increase for that group. The control group was smaller than that of what was used for the autism and Asperger's Syndrome section but the indications spoke volumes. Researchers note that they believe more studying should be done looking into the correlation between maternal smoking and autism.

Swedish Based Study:

A collaboration between Drexel's School of Public Health, Sweden's Karolinska Institute, and the University of Bristol {Bristol, England) looked into whether maternal smoking influenced smoking or not and to see if the past studies suggesting there being a correlation between the two was simply calculating errors.

Researchers involved were:

-Dr. Brian Lee

-Dr. Renee Gardner

-Dr. Henril Dal

-Dr. Anna Svensson

-Dr. Maria Rosaria Galanti

-Dr. Dheeraj Rai

-Dr. Christina Dalman

-Dr. Cecilia Magnusson

Their point was that if you do not compensate for factors like: parental income, education, and job than the numbers are not right. Researchers took information from Sweden registries of right under 4,000 [3,958] autistic children and from right under 39.000 [38,983] children of the same age but without autism. (Lee, 2011) They need the non-autistic children to act as a control group for the findings. The results were: before the adjustment 19.8% of autistic children has mothers that smoked, 18.4% of the control group [non-autistic] had mothers that smoked. These results reflected just what I was talking about, you have to adjust for certain factors. When looking at the initial results, much like previous studies, it suggested that there was a link between the two, however once adjusted the link goes away giving the end result of there not being a link.

I am personally not a big fan of pregnant women smoking, honestly I have some pretty extreme feelings about it, I also have a sister and best friend that smoked during their pregnancies and I love them both, so no judgments to others that did also. Truth is, you shouldn't do it, please don't do it! BUT I suppose it is a good thing that we can delete another possible cause and move the focus on to one of the next on the list.

Chapter 12

Could Meditation be Key in Treating Autism?

Meditation for Autism? When I first said that I was instantly excited! Such a simply powerful thing that's already used to treat many other conditions, disorders, ailments with success.

The Science of Meditation and Autism

Dr. Richard Davidson and Dr. Barbara Fredrickson for the University of Wisconsin study Transcendental meditation and Mindfulness meditation may both be treatment routes to examine. Even though there are differences in these types of meditation they have the same primary objectives of improved cognitive and behavioral functioning. For this study researchers performed EEG's on Buddhist monks as they mediated, the results have proven to be quite interesting ("SaTaNaMa, 2011). It shows that meditating gives most of the same results accredited to ingesting oxytocin. The study goes even further to claim that a person's vagal tone response is strengthened by meditating. Science also suggests that meditating positively helps autistic children by aiding in ("SaTaNaMa, 2011):

-Increasing focus

-Better control of heightened senses

-Self-regulating their emotions

-Decreasing nervousness

-Building better skills to cope with challenges associated with autism

-Increasing the oxytocin levels in the brain

-Increasing empathy

-Strengthening the immune system

-Promoting self-awareness ("SaTaNaMa, 2011)

A 2012 paper written by Sonia Sequeira and Mahiuddin Ahmed with the Memorial Sloan-Kettering Cancer Center in New York speaks of meditation as being "a conscious process of self-regulation that tempers the flow of the thoughts, emotions, and automatic behaviors in the body and mind." They further point out that "neurological disorders that severely impair social integration, professional development, and quality of life have found no solutions in drugs or clinician-facilitated psychology." (Ahmed, 2012) The conclusion of these researcher's findings is that meditation would be beneficial in helping autistic children age 3 to 14 years old; additionally finding that Mantras would also, in fact, be a "feasible intervention" for the smaller children. (Ahmed, 2012) According to said researchers alternative methods should be looked into given the total cost, per individual, for care is $3.2 million over a lifetime and 60-75% of individuals with autism do poorly in adulthood; also because there is only one FDA approved medication for autism, which is Risperidone. (Ahmed, 2012) With this medication there has been no impact shown on autism's core symptoms and is not for use in mild cases.

Chanting mantras ["Aum", "SaTaNaMa"] is nothing new to meditators. However it's now thought that since language, music, and singing all share "functional networks" that, in turn, possibly singing and music could compensate for the deficits in language commonly seen in autistic children (Ahmed, 2012). Chanting mantras is also associated with synching respiratory signals, cerebral blood flow, and cardiovascular rhythms. Currently these researchers are working to implement their own research study to confirm their beliefs.

A Little About Meditation

"Meditation creates a one-pointed mind that helps restore the coherence of the human system as well as harness energy to overcome physical and psychological challenges." (Ahmed, 2012)

It's a cognizant process of blocking out the outside world and of being able to use a certain amount of self-regulation to assuage the movement of our thoughts, instinctive behaviors, and emotions in our body and mind. The Mandukya Upanishad technique teaches us that there are four levels of consciousness from waking to pure consciousness and nineteen channels (Ahmed, 2012):

Photo Courtesy of: Slate.com

-Jagrat(Waking State)

-Svapna (Dreaming State)

-Sudupti (Deep Sleep State)

-Turiya (Pure Consciousness) (Mandukya Upanishad)

-Bhuh-lok

-Svah-lok

-Mahah-lok

-Jana-lok

-Tapah-lok

-Satya-lok (Krishnananda, 2014)

Which include four functions of mind:

-Manas (Work of the Mind)

-Buddhi (Decides and Logically Comes to a Conclusion that something is what it is)

-Ahamkara (Egoism)

-Chitta (Subconscious actions, Memory, Etc.)

Which operate through five pranas (life forces):

-prana (to breathe out)

-apana (to breath in)

-vyana (Circulation of Blood)

-udana (swallowing of food, going into a deep sleep, ego consciousness, and individualized consciousness)

-samana (to digest food)

(The five active senses and the five cognitive senses.)

While scientific findings on using meditation for autism are still few, you have to admit that the findings out there are hopeful. It also has to be said that in most cases the options parents of autistic children are presented with have as little or less research then that which is available for meditation. A great deal of finding the right treatment method is using your gut feelings and experience to determine what to try and what not to try.

There is a great deal of trial and error associated with raising these kids, coming from a parental point of view of course. A big problem for most parents is that several of the few treatment methods available have extreme side effects associated with them. The findings for meditation seem to be quite contrary in comparison, there appears to be no negative side effects as far as this author can find; making it seem even more promising.

All parents of autistic children know that the search for the correct treatment is one of the most challenging things along our journey; this particular method seems to be one of the safest this author has researched or written about. With all the benefits associated with meditating, that have been proven, I don't see why we haven't been doing it longer.

(Price, Could Meditation be Key in Treating Autism?, 2014)

Chapter 13

Stem Cell Treatment and Autism

Some individuals believe stem cell treatments are a form of murder, some believe they are going to save us all. Doctors used stem cells to put an AIDS patient into remission; these cells are amazing. To think that they wouldn't help autism is somewhat naïve. Stem Cells are widely known to be used in the treatment [and in some cases cure] of diseases such as:

-Cystic Fibrosis

-Nerve pain

-Cardiomyopathy

-Parkinson's

-Colon Cancer

(Stem Cell Therapy for Autism, 2007)

All with proven results. How many of you know about treating autism with Mesenchymal Stem Cells and/or CD34+ cord blood cells? I knew nothing until I researched for this, in fact the name 'Mesenchymal' is near unpronounceable in my opinion.

Unquestionably numerous parents have heard of stem cell treatments being used for autism; In turn, unquestionably there are parents that became instantly skeptical, this author sure did. While reading testimonials from parents who had opted to use Stem Cell Treatment on their autistic children interest was definitely aroused.

Parental Claims about Autism Stem Cell Treatment:

The declarations made by parents as to how this treatment helped their children's autism literally made my skin crawl all while giving me faint hope. There aren't any present severity lines in the cases like there are with other treatments. The claims made by parents included children that range from severely autistic [ASD level 3] all the way to the mildest forms [ASD level 1]. Given that information what parent wouldn't be curious when you add it in with reading about the potential to greatly improve things such as their child's:

-Social skills

-Sleep disturbances

-Gross & fine motor skills

-Auditory processing

-Hyperactivity

-Verbal communication issues

-Violent behavior

(Stem Cell Therapy)

A few parents even claimed this treatment literally caused their nonverbal child to speak within days of the first treatment. (Stem Cell Therapy) One thing was for sure, research had to be done; I had to know more about this possibility.

How This Treatment Works:

A 2007 research study charged by:

-Dr. Thomas E. Ichim and Corresponding Author, Neil H. Riordan, both of Medistem Laboratories Inc, Tempe, Arizona

-Dr. Fabio Solano, Dr. Eduardo Glenn, Dr. Frank Morales, and Dr. Leonard Smith, all of the Institute for Cellular Medicine, San Jose, Costa Rica

-Dr. George Zabrecky of the Americas Medical Center, Ridgefield, Connecticut

The base claim is that once administered the umbilical stem cells travel throughout the autistic child's body searching for damaged cells and tissue. (Stem Cell Therapy for Autism, 2007) Once the stem cells find an area of damage they attempt to repair it, leading to the results listed above.

The actual treatment involves taking donor umbilical stem cells, called Mesenchymal Stem Cells [and at times donor Cord blood cells, called CD34+] and administering them to an autistic patient. There are three different ways to administer the stem cells, they are intravenously, subcutaneously, or intrathecally. (Stem Cell Therapy for Autism, 2007) None of which sound like very fun ways to treat an autistic child. I loathe having to take my son into a facility to have an IV put in, let alone to have his skin cut open or fluid put into his spine daily for a week. Scary thoughts, but I digress.

The typical treatment can be administered on one of these three schedules and usually takes about an hour:

Monday- Friday [One week]

-4 intravenous infusion of allogeneic mesenchymal stem cells

Monday-Friday [One week]

-2 intravenous infusions of allogeneic mesenchymal stem cells

-2 intrathecal infusions of allogeneic mesenchymal stem cells

Monday-Friday [Two weeks]

-2 intravenous infusions of allogeneic mesenchymal stem cells

-2 intrathecal infusions of allogeneic mesenchymal stem cells

-1 intravenous infusion of allogeneic mesenchymal stem cells

-1 intrathecal infusion of allogeneic mesenchymal stem cells

(Stem Cell Therapy)

Apparently, distinct from other types of stem cells, with allogeneic mesenchymal stem cells there is no danger of the child's body rejecting the stem cells given to them. This is owed to the fact that these types of cells have no antigenicity. (Stem Cell Therapy for Autism, 2007) This remarkable attribute eradicates the need to use certain drugs that suppress the immune system and can be needed with some stem cell treatments. Cord blood, or CD34+, is known to stimulate living/normal cells and tissue causing them to work at a higher level of functioning.

No matter how well known or unknown, the fact is that this treatment is used worldwide. Stem Cell Treatment is being thoroughly studied from the U.S. to China to India. It has been all the way back to 2007 or before it seems. China did their own study, India currently treats autistic children with stem cell treatments, and the U.S.A. is still doing research studies as well as treatments at certain facilities. As of 2012 The Sutter Neuroscience Institute in California was recruiting for a study using autistic children with already banked cord blood instead of using donor cells.

Even given all this information it is still hard for this author to cope with how extensive the treatment can be. It seems like so much to put our children through in order to help them function. Then again, when compared to hearing your child's first word after years of never hearing their voice or suddenly being able to sit in a room with your child without a violent outburst, possibly even when compared to suddenly gaining the ability to sleep a night without fighting your child to sleep, or even when you compare it all to your child being able to:

-Hold a pencil for the first time

-Tie their own shoe

-Dress themselves

Then all of a sudden the amount of inconvenience associated with Stem Cell Treatments and the possible pain your child may feel for a short time could start to look like it's possibly worth it; I suppose it depends on the situation and the type of parent in said situation. This author believes that this may be the beginning of something very promising. It seem for now we will all just have to wait and see.

(Price, Stem Cell Treatment for Autism May Open Door to a More Promising Future, 2014)

Chapter 14

Maternal and Paternal Depression, Use of Antidepressants and Autism

A Swedish study done between 2001 and 2007 looked into the link between autism and mothers OR fathers who took antidepressants during the pregnancies.

The researchers involved were:

-Dr. Dheeraj Rai

-Dr. Brain Lee

-Dr. Christina Dalman

-Dr. Jean Golding

-Dr. Glyn Lewis

-Dr. Cecilia Magnusson

(Rai, 2013)

The study consisted of 4429 children with autism [1828 with and 2601 without intellectual disability] and 43277 age and sex matching control children. To make this work they matched each autistic child up with 10 control children. (Rai, 2013)They were primarily looking for a correlation between the autistic children and their mothers or fathers taking medication of their depression [SSRI's] and for mothers that had depression listed on the pre-birth paperwork. (Rai, 2013)

Other than an autism diagnosis these researchers all used the following to come to a conclusion, based on their association with autism:

-Maternal age

-Paternal age

-Family income

-Highest level of education by either parent

-Highest occupational class of either parent

-Maternal region of birth

-Parental smoking

-Maternal diabetes or hypertension

-Apgar score

(Rai, 2013)

Regrettably during research the scientist report that in Sweden over 70 percent of mothers were prescribed antidepressants during their pregnancy and that this trend has been going on since 1995. (Rai, 2013) In the end there were very clear, yet somewhat confusing study results.

Of the children and parents looked at, there's no evidence of paternal depression raising the risk of autism in any way, however there is a significant correlation between maternal depression and autism. A depressed mother raises the risk of her child developing autism by 60 percent, they found no significant rise [.6 percent] in risk from the mother taking antidepressants though. (Rai, 2013) The confusing part is that a

California study years back had suggested no maternal depression link and a twofold raise in risk based on taking an SSRI the year before becoming pregnant. It is acknowledged that the difference in findings is likely linked to the vast difference is individuals used in the study. (Rai, 2013)

Chapter 15

Are there Really Environmental Causes of Autism

There are plenty of environmental beliefs concerning the cause of autism. Most still unproven yet still discussed often, others proven, seemingly without a doubt. Researchers have taken on the task of looking into the probability of a child being autistic from various elements. Here's a look into a few of them.

Traffic-Related Air Pollution

A collaborative study between a number of doctors and several establishments is 2013 looked into the relationship between autism and exposure to traffic pollutants. The study was conducted by:

-Dr. Heather E. Volk, PhD, MPH: Departments of Preventive Medicine and Pediatrics, Keck School of Medicine, Zilkha Neurogenetic Institute, and Children's Hospital Los Angeles

-Fred Lurmann: Sonoma Technology, Inc, Petaluma, California

-Bryan Penfold: Sonoma Technology, Petaluma, California

-Irva Hertz-Picciotto, PhD: University of California, Davis

-Dr. Rob McConnell, MD: Departments of Preventitive Medicine and Pediatrics, Keck School of Medicine

The group of researchers looked into 279 children with autism and 245 that were typically developing [control group]. All of these children were enrolled in an environmental study out of California. Researchers looking at the addresses listed on the children's birth certificates, along with the addresses given when enrolling in the Child hood Autism Risks from Genetics and the Environment study [CHARGE]. (Volk, 2013)These types of studies are referred to as "case-control studies".

This study was rather thorough. The took wind speed and direction, atmospheric stability, roadway geometry, link-based traffic volumes, vehicle emission rates, and mixing heights into

account for every child used for the study. (Volk, 2013) In the end the findings were pretty substantial.

-Regional exposure of nitrogen dioxide and particulate matter is

Image Courtesy of Bing Images

associated with autism while mother is pregnant

-Being exposed to nitrogen dioxide during the first year of life is a cause of autism

-Being exposed to nitrogen dioxide, PM2.5 and PM10 during pregnancy and during the first year of life is associated with autism

(Volk, 2013)

As Dr. Volk said herself, "This work has broad public health implications, we've known for a long time that air pollution is bad for our lungs, especially for children. We're now beginning to understand how air pollution may affect the brain." (AutismSpeaks)

Couldn't say it any clearer myself: Being exposed to traffic pollutants during pregnancy and during the first year of life is associated with autism and we are starting to completely understand why and how.

Living Next to a Farm, Can Pesticides Really Cause Autism?

Understandably living next to a farm, or anywhere near one, isn't going to be the only source of pesticides that a pregnant woman can come in contact with. I am from a small farming town in the Midwest so my mind always goes to the corn fields.

As mentioned before, CHARGE [the Childhood Autism Risks for Genetics and Environment Study] was used in this particular study to assess the prevalence of autism in the areas that were reported as using pesticides to the California Pesticide Use Report (1997-2008).

The researchers involved were:

-*Dr. Janie Shelton* of the Department of Public Health Sciences, University of California Davis, Davis, California

-*Dr. Estella M. Geraghty* of the Division of General Medicine, School of Medicine, University of California Davis, Sacramento, California

-*Dr. Daniel J. Tancredi* of the Department of Pediatrics, School of Medicine, University of California Davis and the Center for Healthcare Policy and Research, School of Medicine, University of California Davis

-*Dr. Lora Delwiche* of the Department of Public Health Sciences, University of California Davis, Davis, California

-*Dr. Rebecca Schmidt* of the Department of Public Health Sciences, University of California Davis, Davis, California

-*Dr. Beate Ritz* of the Departments of Epidemiology and the Environmental Health Sciences and Neurology, Fielding School of Public Health and School of Medicine, University of California

-*Dr. Robin Hansen* of the Department of Pediatrics, School of Medicine, University of California, Davis, Sacramento, California and the UC Davis Medical Investigations of Neurodevelopmental Disorders (MIND) Institute, Sacramento, California

-*Dr, Irva Hertz-Picciotto* of the UC Davis Medical Investigations of Neurodevelopmental Disorders (MIND) Institute, Sacramento, California and the Department of Public Health Sciences, University of California Davis, Davis, California

They used 970 individuals that had addresses linked to said report. Then the researchers looked at what type of pesticide and the quantity used within certain distances within each home. The active ingredients found were things such as Organophophates, organochlorines, pyrethroids, and carbamates. (Janie F. Shelton)

Approximately 486 cases of confirmed autism were found and 168 cases of developmental delays. 316 of the individuals were typical developing. When you break it down it shows that 1/3rd of mothers that lived just under a mile from where pesticides were used gave birth to children later diagnosed with autism. (Janie F. Shelton) This study breaks it down even further to show that:

-Living close to organophoshates raises the risk of your child being diagnosed with autism a ridiculous 60 percent!

-That 60 percent raises even higher if you are in your third trimester

-2nd Trimester exposure of chlorpyifos has a risk percentage of over 60 percent as well

-Children of a mother that lives near pyrethroid insecticide just before conception or during the 3rd trimester are at a great risk of being diagnosed with autism

-A raised risk of Developmental Delay was observed neighboring carbamate, but they state that they were unable to determine a "vulnerable period"

(Janie F. Shelton)

This study indubitably adds credibility to the claims that pesticides are a cause of autism, it does not prove it though. Further research will must be done to get to that point. This is a great start with a shocking conclusion, in my opinion.

Chapter 16

Are Twins the Answer to Researching Autism?

This one is undeniably fascinating. Ian Project researchers started looking into twins with an autism diagnoses, whether it be both of the twins or just one. Being able to do autism research that involves twins is simply staggering.

The researchers involved were:

-Dr. Rebecca E. Rosenberg, MD, MPH of the Department of Medical Informatics, Kennedy Krieger Institute

-Dr. Paul A. Law, MD, MPH of the Department of Medical Informatics and the Johns Hopkins Medical Institutions Departments of Pediatrics

-Dr. Gayane Yenokyan, MS of the Johns Hopkins University School of Medicine and Department of Biostatistics; Bloomberg School of Public Health, The Johns Hopkins University Baltimore, Maryland.

-Dr. John McGready, PhD of The Johns Hopkins University School of Medicine and Department of Biostatistics, Bloomberg School of Public Health, The Johns Hopkins University Baltimore, Maryland.

-Dr. Walter E. Kaufmann, MD of the and Center for Genetic Disorders of Cognition and Behavior, Kennedy Jrieger Institute and the Johns Hopkins Medical Institutions Departments of Psychiatry, Neurology, Pathology, and Radiology

-Dr. J. Kiely Law, MD MPH of the Department of Medical Informatics, Kennedy Krieger Institute and the Johns Hopkins Medical Institutions Departments of Pediatrics

(Rebecca E. Rosenberg, et al., 2009)

This study was an internet based study [IANPROJECT] that looked at twins and autism. They wanted, in part, to find out how many identical twins there were that had both twins with an autism diagnosis. Ultimately they looked into 277 twin pairs, 210 which where dizygotic [DZ] and 67 were monozygotc [MZ] that were all 18 or under and one of the twins were autistic. (Rebecca E. Rosenberg, et al., 2009)

In the end the researchers concluded several things:

-ASD concordance [both twins diagnosed with autism] in DZ twins sat at about 31 percent whereas it says at 88 percent for MZ twins

-Male MZ twins had a 100 percent concordance

-Female MZ twins had an 86 percent concordance

-Female DZ twins had a 20 percent concordance where Male DZ twins has a 40 percent concordance

-Affected DZ twins had earlier concern rates from parents (the age when we all sit back and start wondering what is going on) they are also more likely to be diagnosed with an intellectual disability

-MZ twins had a higher prevalence of bipolar disorder and Asperger's syndrome at a higher concordance

(Rebecca E. Rosenberg, et al., 2009)

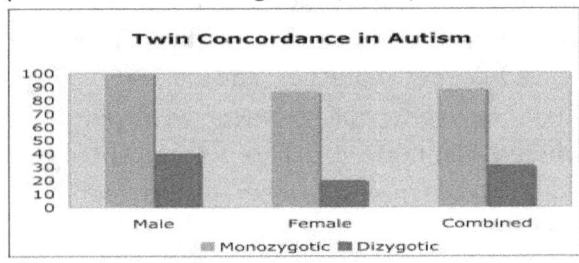

Picture Courtesy of Brainposts.blogspot.com

Overall the study is saying that identical twins have a higher concordance ratio than fraternal twins do. Also it points out that identical twins [where only one twin is diagnosed] are extremely unlikely to see the second twin diagnosed if it is beyond 12 months after the initial diagnosis of the first twin. This study isn't the only one though. There's been a few studies that looked into the autism-twin relationship.

-A 1985 UCLA study looked in to 40 twin sets with only autism. They found that 95.7 percent [22 out of 23 pairs] of identical twins both had an ASD; It suggested that only 23.5 percent [4 out of 17 twin pairs] of fraternal twins both had autism

-A 1989 study from the University of Goteburg, Sweden looked at 21 sets of twins with only autism and concluded that 91 percent [10 out of 11 pairs] of identical twins both has an ASD; it also concluded that 0 percent of fraternal twins both had autism

-A 2008 study from the Nagoya Child Welfare Center, Japan looked at 45 twin sets with Autism, PDD-NOS, and Asperger's and concluded that about 94.7 percent [18 out of 19 pairs] of identical twins both have an ASD; it also concluded that 30.8 percent [8 out of 26 pairs] of fraternal twins both had an ASD

(Iancommunity, 2014)

Researchers now think that twins are going to be key to understanding and researching autism in a way that'll make a bigger impact, leave a deeper impression, and make a considerable difference. Typical siblings only share 50 percent of their genes whereas identical twins share 100 percent of their genes, making research involving them so much more edifying.

Chapter 17

The Ignorant Measures taken to Avoid Autism

The fear of autism has hit a new level of hysteria as of late. Fertility clinics in several countries are allowing parents to select the sex of their babies, and get this, the parents that are choosing this route and also choosing to disregard their boy embryos prior to IVF due to the fear of autism. Their main platform is that the prevalence in boys is 1 in 63 whereas the prevalence in girls is 1 in 189.

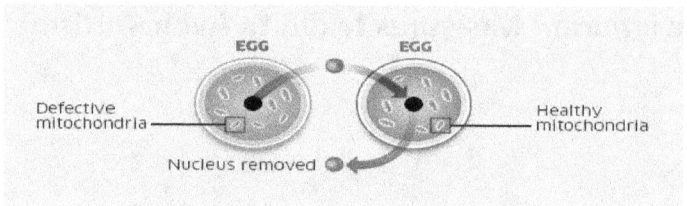

Image Courtesy of ProsperityPharmacy.com

There is an enormous controversy surrounding whether or not IVF is a cause of some cases of autism, so I get the fear, but to pay up to 6000 euros to prevent something from happening than may not in fact occur is sad to me; not to mention that they are paying for a procedure to reduce the risk of autism by using a method that, itself, has been researched as to be a cause.

I couldn't imagine my life without my sons, autistic or not, they are simply remarkable, so thinking of throwing my oldest away because he is different actually makes me sick to my stomach. This could effectively wipe out or spread the autism "epidemic". Only time will tell.

These babies have been nicknamed "designer babies". Parents aren't only disregarding the make embryos due to autism, things such as Duchenne Muscular Dystrophy and Haemophilia are also concerns being addressed in this fashion. Even the doctor doing these procedures (Professor Joy Delhanty of the University College London) said, "It is a reasonable use of technology. It is reducing the risk [of autism] of these families. They were referred to us after undergoing genetic counselling because the families already have one autistic child". (Marsh) To me that makes it even worse.

In contrast, the National Autistic Society had quite different to say, "We are surprised as an organization that sex selection tests are being used as a basis to decide whether a baby may have autism. Having a female does not guarantee a child free of autism." Mr.David King, coordinator of Human Genetics Alert, said: "These kind of techniques should only be offered where the baby is going to suffer a genetic condition that will lead to a short, painful life. That does not apply to autism, and this is the slippery slope towards eugenics." (Marsh) One hundred percent in agreement.

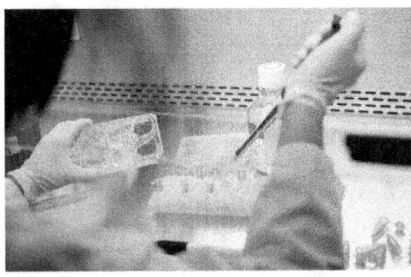

Image Courtesy of Bing Images

I do hope that parents realize they are trying to kill off a group of people over possible medical expenses, personal stress, and stigmas (while I also suspect a tad of embarrassment) of these children. How selfish is that? Autistic children walk into your life, and whether verbal or not, leave you in a state of admiration and awe. While one of the hardest jobs I have ever had, raising my son has been the most rewarding experience imaginable. These kids become your heart, your motivation, and your hero; so, tell me why anyone would want to "run" from that?

Chapter 18

We'll Never Really Know

The sad thing is, I fully believe we will never really have a clue as to what half of the causes of autism are.

Indisputably we will figure out several more, but not all. We do have some really good ideas, along with some really off ones. A couple of the "potential causes" are actually comical, but, can we afford a comical cause? In my opinion I don't care what any of the causes are, once proven, as long as they are just that: proven.

Potential Causes of Autism:

-Refrigerator Moms

-Copy number variants.

-Fluoride

-Percholate

-Bisphenol

-Trichloroethylene

-Microbial infections, both maternal and during infancy

-Gluten and Casein intolerance

-Thimerosol

-Combination of environmental factors and genetic pre-disposition

-Phase of Evolution

-Proximity to freeways

-Hybridization of Human DNA with Dolphin DNA

-Being an Extraterrestrial

-Being a direct descendent of Neanderthals

-Sexual selection

-Use of technology

-Extra DNA strands (not just genes)

-Demonic possession

-Standing near microwaves while pregnant

-Laziness

-Position during conception

-Lipstick and other make-up

-Amalgam fillings

-Mold exposure

-Formula as an infant

-Television

-Mother eating cheese while breastfeeding

-Eating food cooked as opposed to raw

-Difference in intestinal length

-Differences in brain structure

-Being so smart the brain short circuits

-Being an angel

-Mother dying hair while pregnant

(Sidther)

The last 7 years or so researchers have made incredible advances in autism research, this book includes the work of some of the best scientists and doctors in the world; all extremely impressive contributions to the autism movement. When thought about I cannot wait to see what the next 7-20 years bring. Could we have a cause, a cure? How about just a few answers? What if parents continue to gender select, will there be no more autistic children? The possibilities and nightmares one could think of are endless.

About the Author

Brooke is 30 years old and from Indiana. She currently lives in Seattle, WA. She's been married for 11 years. Brooke is the mother of 2 beautiful little boys. Her oldest son is autistic. He was not diagnosed until he was 5, didn't speak until almost age 7.

Brooke is also a co-administrator of an online autism support group. She fought for her son for years to get to the point of having some stability in his condition and now wants to help other parents understand this disorder. Brooke hopes that by publishing this book she will be able to bring hope and some awareness to the plight of the autistic child and their parent(s). She hopes to comfort some and open the eyes of others.

Sample of

"Living Through Autism's Eyes: My Journey with My Son"

Chapter One

The Beginning

I had known Chaz Price for a long time once we started dating when I was 17. We had been friends for a while and I had never thought that we would end up together, but we had. On December 7th, 2002 we were married in a semi small ceremony in front of our family and a few friends. I was so in love and so happy. We had so much fun together and I was looking forward to our life together more and more every day. A few months after we were married we found out we were going to be parents. We were scared but so excited at the same time. And on November 19, 2003 my husband and my life's changed forever. We became parents for the first time.

We had planned diligently for our son's arrival. Read every book we could, decorated his room in care bears, safety guarded the house for, what we thought, was every threat possible. We were ready for this change, we were excited. I remember sitting at night together and talking about what he would look like, what he would be like-surely a character with a great sense of humor & tons of friends, and what he would do when he got older. Basically putting all our dreams for our new son out there. Little did we know, all the precautions we took, all the talks we had, all the books we read, everything we did to ready ourselves for parenthood were for not. No one on this earth could've prepared us for the changes we were about to face. Nobody prepared us for if there was something wrong. Nobody prepared us for if he was disabled. I didn't read any books about that.

At 8:06 pm, November 19th, Zain Mikeal was born. I pictured his birth through my whole pregnancy. He'd arrive. Chaz would cut his cord. Zain would cry his first cry. We would all cry as well. I'd feed him for the first time. Pretty much standard. His birth was nothing like this, and little did I know then, his birth would scar me for years to come.

I pushed my precious child out, Chaz cut his cord, and then nothing, and still nothing. No cries, no handing my baby to me. It was silent. I remember looking over and Chaz was frantic, standing by the warming table. I was utterly confused as to why my sister, Shelena, had stopped filming. It felt like I was in a dream. I was out of it because of the epidural, so the gravity of this situation didn't hit me until later. Plus nobody came right out and told me my son was not breathing. For the next 6 minutes I am sure it felt like the world stopped for my husband. I know if I had comprehended it fully I would've been losing it, so I have to give him serious props for holding it together for me.

Finally at 8:12 pm we heard Zain cry for the first time. We were parents. He was 8 pounds 1 ounce and 22 inches of beautiful. He had blue eyes from the start and blond hair. Holding him put my heart at peace for the first time in my life. I felt complete. He was beautiful. I have been lucky enough to feel that feeling twice in my life, there is nothing like it. Zain seemed fine, we were all relieved. Until 2 days later.

On November 21, 2003 I was brought my son in the middle of the night to feed. I was alone and very scared, like first day of kindergarten scared, or first day of a new job scared. Chaz had to go home that night to return to work, which I didn't oppose, but didn't like either. I tried and tried to get Zain to latch on, but he wouldn't. I sat there and stared at him trying to figure out what to do and ultimately feeling like a failure. I noticed he was 'twitching' so hard that I thought maybe that is why he wouldn't latch on for anything. This wasn't really a 'twitch', but I have no other words to describe what my newborn was doing. I had never seen anything like this before, ever! I buzzed the nurse and she told me it was normal for newborns to twitch some. I tried to believe her, I tried to chalk up this 'twitching' to just normal newborn stuff like she said, but it didn't seem right. I had this feeling in the pit of my stomach. I couldn't just let it go. It didn't take me 10 minutes after buzzing them that I was buzzing back frantic. I didn't know what was going on, but I needed help. He wouldn't stop this 'twitching'. The nurse came, took one look at him laying between my legs, grabbed him and ran. She didn't even take his bassinet, just him, and ran!

~Hope you enjoyed the first half of the first chapter of "Living Through Autism's Eyes: My Journey with my Son"~

References

"SaTaNaMa, ". (2011, July 24). *Meditation and Autism.*
    Retrieved from http://www.autismkey.com:
    http://www.autismkey.com/meditation-and-autism/

2013, N. (n.d.). *Copy Number Variations.* Retrieved from
    University of Toronto:
    http://neurowiki2013.wikidot.com/individual:copy-
    number-variations

22 Main Autism Symptoms. (n.d.). Retrieved from Asperger-
    Symptoms: http://www.autism-symptoms.net

AGRE. (n.d.). *PROGRAM DESCRIPTION.* Retrieved from
    https://research.agre.org:
    https://research.agre.org/program/descr.cfm

Ahmed, S. S. (2012). *Meditation as a Potential Therapy for
    Autism: A Review.* Retrieved from
    http://www.hindawi.com:
    http://www.hindawi.com/journals/aurt/2012/835847/

APP. (n.d.). *Autism Phenome Project (APP) and Autism Genetic
    Resource Exchange (AGRE).* Retrieved from
    www.ucdmc.ucdavis.edu:
    http://www.ucdmc.ucdavis.edu/mindinstitute/research
    /app/

*Arbaclofen Shows Promise for Treating Core Symptoms of
    Autism.* (2012). Retrieved from Autism Speaks:
    http://www.autismspeaks.org/science/science-
    news/top-ten-lists/2012/arbaclofen-shows-promise-
    treating-core-symptoms-autism

AutismSpeaks. (n.d.). *Deeper Understanding of Link between
    Chemical Pollutants and Autism.* Retrieved from
    http://www.autismspeaks.org:

http://www.autismspeaks.org/science/science-news/top-ten-lists/2012/deeper-understanding-link-chemical-pollutants-and-autism

Brooks, M. (2012, June 1). *Oxytocin Nasal Spray May Improve Social Function in Autism*. Retrieved from medscape.com: http://www.medscape.com/viewarticle/764903

CDC. (2014). *Autism and Developmental Disabilities Monitoring (ADDM) Network*. Retrieved from CDC.gov: http://www.cdc.gov/ncbddd/autism/addm.html

CDC. (n.d.). *CDC's Autism and Developmental Disabilities Monitoring (ADDM) Network*. Retrieved from Centers for Disease Control and Prevention: http://www.cdc.gov/ncbddd/autism/states/addm-fact-sheet_508.pdf

CHARGE. (n.d.). *Welcome.* Retrieved from CHARGE: http://beincharge.ucdavis.edu/

Conneely, M. M. (n.d.). *Oxytocin improves social skills in children with autism*. Retrieved from advocacyinactionireland: http://advocacyinactionireland.blogspot.com/2013/12/oxytocin-improves-social-skills-in.html

Drugs & Medications. (n.d.). Retrieved from WebMD: http://www.webmd.com/drugs/drug-63499-oxytocin+nasal.aspx?drugid=63499&drugname=oxytocin+nasal&source=2&pagenumber=6

EM, B.-K. (2012, September 19). *Effects of STX209 (arbaclofen) on neurobehavioral function in children and adults with fragile x syndrome: a randomized, controlled, phase 2 trial* . Retrieved from US National Library of Medicine

Nationsl Institiutes of Health:
http://www.ncbi.nlm.nih.gov/pubmed/22993294

Gardner, F. (2013, October 22). *Comes Now Epidiolex™ (FDA approves IND studies of CBD)*. Retrieved from www.beyondthc.com: http://www.beyondthc.com/comes-now-epidiolex-fda-approves-ind-studies-of-cbd/

Groce, V. (2014, May 19). *Foods with Gluten*. Retrieved from About.com: http://foodallergies.about.com/od/wheatallergies/qt/glutenfreediet.htm

Gul Dolen, A. D. (2012, November 26). *Social reward requires coordinated activity of nucleus accumbens oxytocin and serotonin*. Retrieved from Nature: http://www.nature.com/nature/journal/v501/n7466/full/nature12518.html

Hughes, M. (n.d.). *Mild Autism Symptoms*. Retrieved from eHow: http://www.ehow.com/facts_4812453_mild-autism-symptoms.html

Iancommunity. (2014, August 21). *TWINS! A KEY TO THE MYSTERIES OF AUTISM*. Retrieved from http://www.iancommunity.org: http://www.iancommunity.org/cs/ian_research_reports/ian_research_report_oct_2009

IanProject. (2008, November 11). *Ian Research Findings: Special Diets*. Retrieved from Ian Research: http://www.iancommunity.org/cs/ian_research_reports/treatment_series_special_diets

IANProject. (n.d.). *What is Ian Research*. Retrieved from Iancommunity.org:

http://www.iancommunity.org/cs/ian_research/overvie
w

Institute, K. K. (n.d.). *Interactive Autism Network Project*.
    Retrieved from http://www.kennedykrieger.org:
    http://www.kennedykrieger.org/research-
    training/current-research-projects/funded-
    research/interactive-autism-network-project

Iyer, S. (2014, July 7). *What Causes Autism? Rare Mutation In
    The CHD8 Gene May Be Responsible For Autism
    Subtype*. Retrieved from medicaldaily.com:
    http://www.medicaldaily.com/what-causes-autism-
    rare-mutation-chd8-gene-may-be-responsible-autism-
    subtype-291602

Janie F. Shelton, E. M.-P. (n.d.). *Neurodevelopmental Disorders
    and Prenatal Residential Proximity to Agricultural
    Pesticides: The CHARGE Study*. Retrieved from
    http://ehp.niehs.nih.gov/:
    http://ehp.niehs.nih.gov/1307044/

Kalkbrenner, A. E. (2012, April 25). *Maternal Smoking during
    Pregnancy and the Prevalence of Autism Spectrum
    Disorders, Using Data from the Autism and
    Developmental Disabilities Monitoring Network*.
    Retrieved from http://www.ncbi.nlm.nih.gov:
    http://www.ncbi.nlm.nih.gov/pmc/articles/PMC340466
    3/?report=classic

Krishnananda, S. (2014). *The Mandukya Upanishad*. Retrieved
    from http://www.swami-krishnananda.org:
    http://www.swami-krishnananda.org/disc/disc_74.html

Lee, B. K. (2011, September). *Brief Report: Maternal Smoking
    During Pregnancy and Autism Spectrum Disorders*.
    Retrieved from http://link.springer.com:

http://link.springer.com/article/10.1007/s10803-011-1425-4#page-1

Low Functioning Autism . (n.d.). Retrieved from BrightTots : http://www.brighttots.com/Autism/Low_Functioning_Autism.html

Mandukya Upanishad. (n.d.). Retrieved from http://en.wikipedia.org: http://en.wikipedia.org/wiki/Mandukya_Upanishad

Marsh, B. (n.d.). *Baby selection fear.* Retrieved from dailymail.com: http://www.dailymail.co.uk/health/article-159671/Baby-selection-fear.html

MIND, U. D. (n.d.). *Built by families for families.* Retrieved from UCDAVIS MIND INSTITUTE: http://www.ucdmc.ucdavis.edu/mindinstitute/aboutus/index.html

Negro, M.-P. (n.d.). *"Growing up with Fragile X".* Retrieved from fragilexproject.com: http://fragilexproject.wordpress.com/

NLM. (n.d.). *The ScanBrit randomised, controlled, single-blind study of a gluten- and casein-free dietary intervention for children with autism spectrum disorders.* Retrieved from biomedsearch.com: http://www.biomedsearch.com/nih/ScanBrit-randomised-controlled-single-blind/20406576.html

No oxytocin benefit for autism. (2013, July 18). Retrieved from UNSW Australia: https://newsroom.unsw.edu.au/news/science/no-oxytocin-benefit-autism

PDD-NOS Signs, Symptoms, and Treatment. (n.d.). Retrieved from National Autism Resources: http://www.nationalautismresources.com/autismsympt oms.html

Plus, M. (n.d.). *Dronabinol.* Retrieved from www.nlm.nih.gov: http://www.nlm.nih.gov/medlineplus/druginfo/meds/a 607054.html

Price, B. (2014, July 16). *Cause for autism sub-type found: what does this mean for parents? .* Retrieved from emaxhealth.com: http://www.emaxhealth.com/1257/autism-sub-type-cause-found-parents-what-to-do

Price, B. (2014, July 16). *Could Meditation be Key in Treating Autism?* Retrieved from emaxhealth.com: http://www.emaxhealth.com/1257/meditation-autism-treatment-key

Price, B. (2014, June 2). *Does the Gluten Free-Casein Free DIet Have a Place in the Autism Community?* Retrieved from emaxhealth.com: http://www.emaxhealth.com/12577/gluten-free-casein-free-diet-place-autism-community

Price, B. (2014, August 20). *Ever wondered how they come up with Autism Prevalence Numbers?* Retrieved from emaxhealth.com: http://www.emaxhealth.com/1/ever-wondered-how-they-come-autism-prevalence-numbers

Price, B. (2014, May 19). *Stem Cell Treatment for Autism May Open Door to a More Promising Future.* Retrieved from emaxhealth.com: http://www.emaxhealth.com/12577/autism-stem-cell-therapy-treatment-parents-claim

Price, B. (2014, July 26). *What's in a name? Changes in Autism Severity*. Retrieved from Emaxhealth.com: http://www.emaxhealth.com/1257/autism-severity-whats-in-name

Price, B. (2014, May 27). *Will oxytocin nasal spray treatments for autism really work?* . Retrieved from emaxhealth.com: http://www.emaxhealth.com/12577/oxytocin-nasal-spray-treatment-autism-work

Rai, D. (2013, April 19). *Parental depression, maternal antidepressant use during pregnancy, and risk of autism spectrum disorders: population based case-control study.* Retrieved from the bmj: http://www.bmj.com/content/346/bmj.f2059

Raphael Bernier, C. G. (2014, July 17). *Disruptive CHD8 Mutations Define a Subtype of Autism Early in Development.* Retrieved from Cell: http://www.cell.com/cell/abstract/S0092-8674%2814%2900749-1

Rebecca E. Rosenberg, M. M., J. Kiely Law, M. M., Gayane Yenokyan, M., John McGready, P., Walter E. Kaufmann, M., & Paul A. Law, M. M. (2009, October 05). *Characteristics and Concordance of Autism Spectrum Disorders Among 277 Twin Pairs* . Retrieved from http://archpedi.jamanetwork.com: http://archpedi.jamanetwork.com/article.aspx?articleid=382225

Researchers launch study with oxytocin nasal spray. (n.d.). Retrieved from Autismspeaks: http://www.autismspeaks.org/science/science-news/researchers-launch-study-oxytocin-nasal-spray

Reversal of disease-related pathologies in fragile x mouse model by selectve activation of GABAB receptors with arbaclofen. (2012, September 19). Retrieved from US National Library of Medicine National Institutes of Health: http://www.ncbi.nlm.nih.gov/pubmed/22993295

Sidther. (n.d.). *Strange theories about the causes of Autism .* Retrieved from http://www.squidoo.com/: http://www.squidoo.com/funny-theories-about-the-causes-of-autism

Sonia Sequeira, M. A. (2012). *Meditation as a Potential Therapy for Autism: A Review.* Retrieved from http://www.hindawi.com: http://www.hindawi.com/journals/aurt/2012/835847/

Stem Cell Therapy. (n.d.). Retrieved from Stem Cell Institute: http://www.cellmedicine.com/stem-cell-therapy-for-autism/

Stem Cell Therapy for Autism. (2007, June 27). Retrieved from ncbi.nlm.nih.gov: http://www.ncbi.nlm.nih.gov/pmc/articles/PMC1914111/

Therapeutics, S. (n.d.). *Seaside Therapeutics Publishes Seminal Research Supporting Disease-Modifying Potential of STX209 for the Treatment of Fragile X Syndrome.* Retrieved from BusinessWire: http://www.businesswire.com/news/home/20120919006599/en/Seaside-Therapeutics-Publishes-Seminal-Research-Supporting-Disease-Modifying#.U9iNZ2OB8vk

Thomas Sudhof. (2013). *Autism-Associated Neuroligin-3 Mutations Commonly Disrupt Tonic Endocannabinoid Signaling.* Retrieved from Cell.com:

http://www.cell.com/neuron/fulltext/S0896-
6273%2813%2900225-0

UCI. (n.d.). *Boosting natural marijuana-like brain chemicals
   treats fragile X syndrome symptoms.* Retrieved from
   UCI.edu: http://news.uci.edu/press-releases/boosting-
   natural-marijuana-like-brain-chemicals-treats-fragile-x-
   syndrome-symptoms/

Volk, D. H. (2013, January). *Traffic-Related Air Pollution,
   Particulate Matter, and Autism.* Retrieved from
   http://archpsyc.jamanetwork.com:
   http://archpsyc.jamanetwork.com/article.aspx?articleid
   =1393589

What are the Symptoms of Fragile X Syndrome? . (n.d.).
   Retrieved from Eunoce Kennedy Shriver National
   Institute of Child Health and Human Development:
   http://www.nichd.nih.gov/health/topics/fragilex/condit
   ioninfo/Pages/commonsymptoms.aspx

www.ingramcontent.com/pod-product-compliance
Lightning Source LLC
Chambersburg PA
CBHW070537290526
45790CB00002B/532